CUFF LINKS

© 2002 Assouline Publishing for the present edition
601 West 26th Street, 18th floor
New York, NY 10001
USA
Tel.: 212 989-6810   Fax: 212 647-0005
www.assouline.com

First published by Editions Assouline, Paris, France.

Translated from the French by Ilona Bossanyi
Proofreading: Jennifer Ditsler

Color separation: Gravor (Switzerland)
Printed by Grafiche Milani (Italy)

ISBN: 2 84323 338 0

BERTRAND PIZZIN
JEAN-NOËL LIAUT

CUFF LINKS

FOREWORD BY KARL LAGERFELD

ASSOULINE

Foreword by Karl Lagerfeld

For some reason of which I'm unaware, Germans talk about "having the cuffs" when they're frightened. Being frightened isn't a good thing, but having cuffs certainly is, if only to be able to wear cuff links. Cuff links are one of the very few pieces of jewelry that women have left to men. It's true that men have taken over chains, earrings and large finger rings to give a particular kind of image, but cuff links (and tie pins) have always retained their character as "useful" men's ornaments, although —sadly—their use has been declining. Shirts are increasingly worn without a tie, and shirts with double cuffs are rarely made nowadays (except for evening dress, where I personally prefer stiffly starched single cuffs).

Until the Second World War, cuff links were full of inventiveness and refinement. The jewelry work involved was often of quite remarkable delicacy. Even the simpler, inexpensive cuff links made at the time are worthy of being collector's items today. Any collection is justified by its variety, and a collection that's

4

Karl Lagerfeld, *Self-portrait*, 2001.

worthy of its name—like this one—does not have to include only items signed by Cartier or Fabergé—quite the contrary, in fact. In a collection of this kind, humor is also an important factor.

I've always adored—and worn—shirts with cuffs that are made for cuff links, and I've also been collecting them since I was a child—although I'm not a true collector like Bertrand Pizzin. As a child, I wanted to dress like my father, whose elegance bore the stamp of a bygone age (he was born in 1880), which to me was the only valid reference and to which I have remained profoundly attached to this day. He had kept various pairs of pre-1900 cuff links, and these made up a nice little collection that he seemed to view with the greatest detachment. He nearly always wore the same pair: perhaps there was a story there, a treasured memory—I don't know. He never told it to me, but he left me his collection which became the start of my own. I do have favorite pairs that I wear more often than others, but I change them nearly every day, sometimes twice a day (and even three times if I possibly can), because I'm a bit of a shirt freak. As a fashion designer, I would love to have invented the white shirt, as others would love to have invented jeans.

The items in Bertrand Pizzin's collection are much more than mere objects made for a purpose—they have become witnesses to other times, even to other ways of life. Cuff links have become a curio, and that is also why collecting them is entirely natural. Today, it seems rather old-fashioned to think that an immaculate shirt cuff with a well-chosen pair of cuff links underlines the delicacy of a woman's wrist. Also, the care that a shirt needs to set off a fine pair of cuff links is not so easy to achieve nowadays. The fine laundries that looked after gentlemen's outfits (like the one near Place de la Madeleine in Paris that was still offering such services just ten years ago) have disappeared for want of custom. Although there's little room for such refinement in today's lifestyles, many men who consider their style of dress as "conventional" would look a lot less dull with a pair of fine cuff links at the wrist to relieve the monotony of their shirts, however finely made. Cuff links may well come back into fashion, as all fashions eventually do, often in different forms and different contexts, but meanwhile, it's important to keep their memory alive through collections like this one.

Marlene Dietrich was the only woman who loved, wore and collected cuff links: Dietrich, the very symbol of femininity, who loved one thing above all others during her years of glory—to dress as a man.

Paris, December 2001

To Maria Félix,

In the late 1950s in Paris, during a dinner party given by Arturo Lopez-Willshaw, the "Sun King" of the Café Society, one of the guests, greatly admiring the cuff links worn by her neighbor—a man renowned for his good taste—exclaimed: "How absolutely beautiful! Fabergé?" Pausing enigmatically for effect, the young aesthete replied: "No, Benvenuto Cellini...."
Every piece created by Cellini, the Florentine goldsmith and sculptor (1500–1571) who worked for François I and Cosimo de Medici, has been sought after ever since by the world's great museums. Taking aesthetic fervor to the point of wearing such creations in the form of cuff links says a good deal about the importance a man can give to an ornament that's barely an inch wide and scarcely visible just below the hem of a sleeve. A fervor that Des Esseintes, the hero of Huysman's *A Rebours* and an icon among dandies, would surely have approved—for such elegance truly reflects a sense of self projected through one's attire.

Above: Arturo Lopez at a fancy dress ball given by Elsa Maxwell. Paris, 1952
Opposite: Michael Sweerts, *Portrait of a young man (self-portrait)*, 1656.
Hermitage Museum, Saint Petersburg.

It goes without saying that a man of elegance never wears jewelry, except a wedding ring, a watch, a signet ring bearing his family's arms, and a tie pin. An older or exceptionally refined man might carefully select a knob for his cane. Wearing a gold chain round the neck, a chain bracelet, earrings or finger rings would be tantamount to committing aesthetic and social suicide, at least in the eyes of some circles of western society since the 19th century. And nothing on earth would induce such a man to suffer the voluptuous pain of body piercing. A nose ring! Utterly inconceivable, at least to any 19th-century beau, who, as Stendhal put it, would shudder with an almost hydrophobic horror at the mere sight of crudeness. For any budding Beau Brummell, who is secretly fascinated by precious stones and rare materials, cuff links are the only possible alternative.

Cuff links first appeared in Europe in the early years of the 17th century but were rarely used, as the dandies of the time preferred lace and ribbons to hold their shirt cuffs. Metal was for sabres and spurs —often true masterpieces of craftsmanship—and only a few eccentrics might use gold or silver buttons with a fine chain link.

Above: Nathaniel Hone, *Portrait of Sir John Fielding*
(detail), 1762. National Gallery, London.

Emeralds, rose-cut diamonds,
yellow gold. Late 18th century.

By the end of that century, a few pairs of cuff links were being created in zircon crystals that imitated diamonds to perfection, or in *strass*—invented by a native of Strasbourg, hence its name—a synthetic gem that enabled impecunious dandies to satisfy the taste for gemstones that swept through the royal courts of Europe at the time. The truly fanatical dandies, such as the Duke of Chartres or the Duke of Penthièvre to name but two, even insisted on having their buttonholes embroidered with real diamonds.

It was not until the 19th century that cuff links really came into their own. Various factors were at work, like changes in the styling of men's shirts brought about by the industrial revolution, which meant they could be produced much more cheaply. After the French Revolution, the splendid originality of 18th-century masculine wardrobes gave way—in France and England at least—to democratic sobriety under the "reign" of Beau Brummell, whose influence, even well after his death, remained omnipresent across Europe and the New World throughout the 19th century.

Aristocratic magnificence was sacrificed to the bourgeois efficiency of the new business class. And, as Barbey d'Aurevilly deplored in the columns of *Le Constitutionnel* on 13 October 1845, "a salon of black-clad men always seems to emanate the tedium of a Methodist congregation at a sermon."

Above: J. Testevuide, *George Brummell.*
Opposite: Louis Gauffier, *Young Man near Vesuvius, late 18th century.*

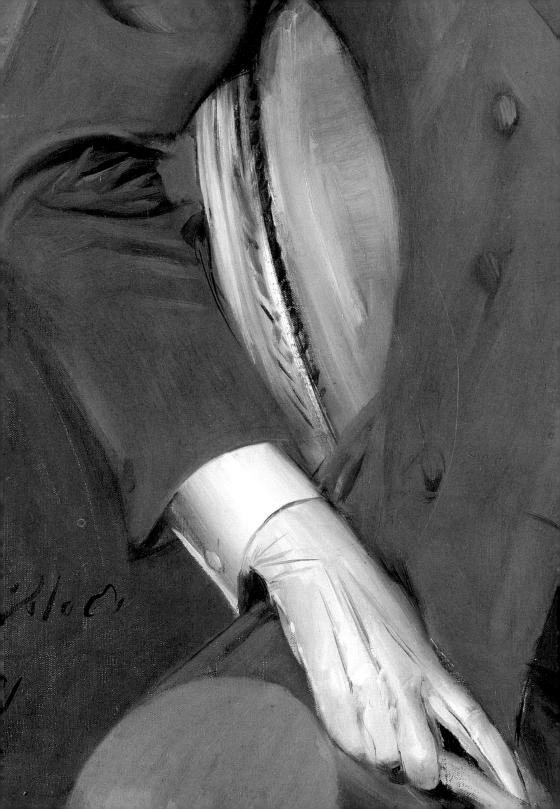

Even the dandies and young romantics, venerating beauty and despising the vulgarity of a society in thrall to the quest for lucre, were less than audacious in their attire. And what of the bankers and bureaucrats of the Second Empire?

With very few exceptions—like the "petits crevés" (the dead-beats), a small band of eccentrics thus nicknamed for their permanent state of exhaustion induced by endless partying—men generally wore a dark suit in the daytime and a smoking jacket or tails—both black—in the evening.

This strictly conventional attire was only relieved by cuff links, which, minuscule as they were, became a source of boundless inspiration for their designers. The rich variety of shapes and materials spoke for themselves, as did the numerous and complex fastening devices. There were "chain-links," linking two similar-shaped studs or a stud and toggle, and especially appropriate for town or sportswear, "extendable chain links" to vary the way a cuff could open at the wrist, "rigid links" with a fixed decorative piece attached to a pivoting stud that were more practical than truly elegant, not to mention such inventions as the "swingover stud," the "dual effect stud," the "toggle" or the "press-stud."

GENTS' 14 K GOLD CUFF LINKS.

PRICES PER PAIR.

No. 389. $41.00.
Platinum and Gold.
Diamond Set.

No. 3810. $31.00.
Roman.
Diamond Set.

No. 3811. Polished. $15.00.
No. 3812. Roman. $16.25.
Raised Ornamentation.

No. 3813. $15.25.
Polished.

No. 3814. $14.67.
Polished Gold and Platinum.

No. 3815. $13.50.
Polished.

No. 3816. Polished. $10.75.
No. 3817. Roman. $10.75.

No. 3818. Polished. $9.75.
No. 3819. Roman. $9.75.

SOLID GOLD CUFF LINKS.

PRICES PER PAIR.

No. 391. $7.00.
Roman.

No. 392. $7.00.
Roman.

No. 393. $6.50.
Roman and Polished.

No. 394. $5.00.
Roman and Polished.

No. 395. $4.75.
Roman.

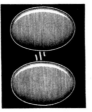

No. 396. $5.25.
Roman.

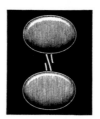

No. 397. $4.50.
Roman.

No. 398. $3.75.
Roman.

Above: Rose-cut diamonds, pearls, yellow gold. Early 19th century.
Opposite: Page from the *Illustrated Jewelry Catalog 1892,*
The New England Jeweler.

17

Above: Enamel, silver gilt. Late 19th century.
Opposite: Henri Fantin-Latour, *A Batignolles Workshop*
(detail), 1870. Musée d'Orsay, Paris.

Advances in jewelry techniques, like electroplating to combine gold or silver with other metals, or the channel setting technique originated by Van Cleef & Arpels that revolutionized the mounting of precious stones—also played a crucial part in the history of cuff links.

But it was through the sheer variety of motifs and materials that the fertile imagination of the designers really came into its own, especially in England. While their least daring customers remained faithful to the family coat of arms or monogram, others—Victorian modesty notwithstanding—would sport Etruscan Medusa heads, Egyptian mosaics or Gothic stained-glass motifs. Influences mingled and combined: a fascination with India, Japan or the Pre-Raphaelite movement, Walter Scott's idealized vision of the Middle Ages, a craze for the art of Antiquity—Bulwer-Lytton's *The Last Days of Pompeii* was a best-seller in the second half of the 19th century— even Celtic myths and legends. The Prince of Wales, later Edward VII, imposed a virile form of dandyism that became as much imitated as his precious pair of Fabergé cuff links.

Above: A caricature of William Waldorf Astor.

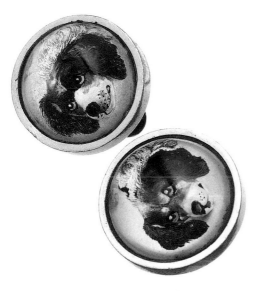

Fixed under glass. England,
late 19th century.

Exotic fruit mounted on silver.
Indian craftsmanship, late 19th century.

Shells mounted on silver.
Late 19th century.

Enamel and silver gilt.
England, circa 1900.

From Cartier to Tiffany, all the great jewelers succumbed to the wave of Anglomania and Art Nouveau that swept through society from the 1880s for over twenty years. Milky opals, moonstones or enamel cloisonné work were much in vogue to reflect the dreamy sensuality of the symbolist poet's ideal woman, whose flower-like face, immortalized by Alphonse Mucha, one of the founding fathers of Art Nouveau, and embodied by Sarah Bernhardt as *Medea* (1898)—ornamented many a man's wrist. The Decorative Arts Exhibition inaugurated on 18 July 1925 in the midst of a maze of scaffolding and immediately nicknamed the "Exposition des Arts décors hâtifs" (literally, the exhibition of hasty artwork), marked a new chapter in the history of cuff links. Influenced by movements as diverse as Cubism, jazz or the Bauhaus, Art Deco was everywhere, from architecture to furnishings and from dress design to jewelry.

Above: Silver. Emile Lavillème, circa 1900.
Opposite: Church of Saint-Jean-l'Evangéliste, Paris.
Anatole de Baudot, 1894-1904.

22

Aventurine, yellow gold.
Circa 1900.

Carnelian, silver.
Italy, circa 1910.

Above: Turquoise, silver gilt. Circa 1900.
Opposite: Museum of Arts and Crafts,
Budapest. Odön Lechner, 1896.

Above: Fixed under glass, silver. Circa 1880.
Opposite: Palace of Catalan music,
Barcelona. lluis Domènech, 1905-1908.

Enamel, yellow gold.
Circa 1900.

Quartz, brilliants,
platinum. Circa 1910.

Mother-of-pearl, pearls,
yellow gold. Circa 1900.

Cabochon sapphire, mother-of-pearl,
yellow gold. Circa 1940.

Blue topaz, brilliants,
yellow gold. Circa 1910.

Above: Agate, silver. Circa 1900.
Opposite: Ankerhaus, Vienna.
Otto Wagner, 1895.

The man of fashion, who saw himself as the "Man with the Hispano," the hero of a best-selling novel by Pierre Frondaie, chose cuff links which, for the first time, came in such unexpected combinations as plastic, leather or chromium with abstract geometric motifs. Shirt cuffs appeared to be adorned with miniature paintings by Sonia Delaunay. The idols of the new age of speed and modernity were sportsmen in natty suits like Charles Lindbergh the aviator or Bobby Jones the golfer, neither of whom would have dreamed of being seen without their cuff links. *O tempora, o mores…*

Throughout the 1920s and 30s, many artists, whose works have now become the pride and joy of museums around the world, brought endless refinements to the art of the cufflink. Among them were the Swiss jeweler Paul Brandt, Louis Féron and Jean Schlumberger—both with Tiffany in New York, Monsieur Boyer of Paris and Fulco di Verdura, an authentic Sicilian duke who had abandoned his splendid but dilapidated ancestral home in Palermo to work as a jeweler. His enamel bracelets ornamented with the Maltese Cross—designed for his good friend Coco Chanel—speak volumes about his inventiveness at a time when ropes of pearls and rivers of diamonds still reigned supreme.

Above: Enamel, silver. Circa 1925.
Opposite: Georges Barbier, *The Judgment of Pâris*. Illustration for
Falbalas et Fanfreluches, a 1924 fashion almanac.

Enamel, grey gold.
Circa 1925.

Enamel, grey gold.
Paul Brandt, circa 1920

Enamel, murat.
Circa 1940.

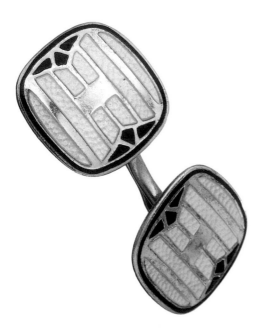

Enamel, silver gilt.
England, circa 1930.

Enamel, silver.
Circa 1930.

37

Diamonds, onyx, white gold.
Circa 1920.

Enamel, silver.
Circa 1920.

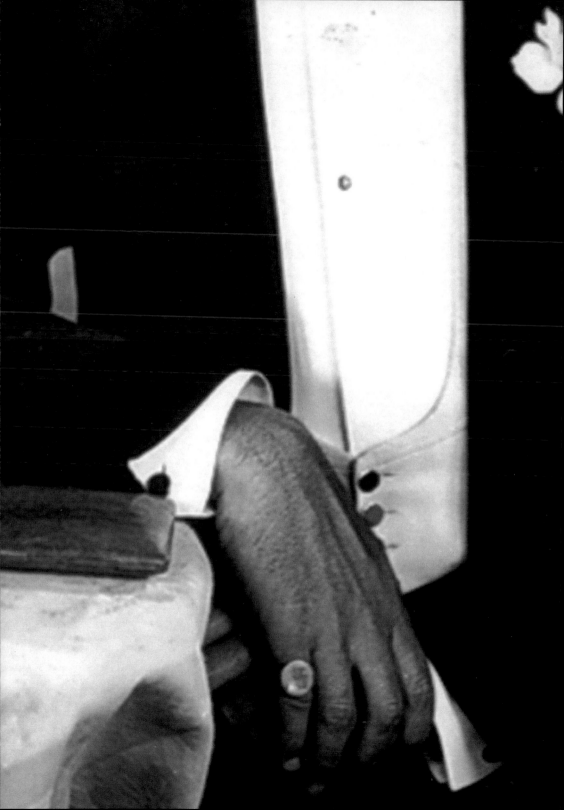

From that time, and until the 1950s and 60s, di Verdura created men's cuff links of wonderful refinement in the shape of animals or flowers, sometimes with real shells encrusted with precious stones mounted in pairs. His friends and clients made up the élite set of the Café Society. Cole Porter, the Duke of Windsor and Cary Grant became his ambassadors, as did a number of society women who would sally forth in masculine suits, ties and cuff links, like the Russian princess Natalie Paley, Tallulah Bankhead, the eccentric heroine of Hitchcock's *Lifeboat*, or Daisy Fellowes. According to legend, the latter—said to be the most elegant human being of the 20th century—commissioned a pair of cuff links from the Duke in the shape of a pair of handcuffs, as an allusion to the passion binding her to one of her lovers.

During the 1930s, other even more famous women also contributed to the popularity of cuff links among their own sex. Marlene Dietrich for one, who wore them in town and on screen, for example as the unforgettable Lola-Lola in the *Blue Angel*, or as Amy Jolly, the heroine of *Morocco*, clad in top hat and tails to sing in a sailors' dive, a cigarette between her fingers, feverishly gesturing hands adorned with mother-of-pearl cuff links—and taking cinema to the heights of eroticism as she kisses a young Spanish girl full on the lips.

Above: Man Ray, *Jean Cocteau*, 1925.
Preceding pages: *After Dinner Drinks* and *In the First Row*.

Amethysts, white gold.
Circa 1920.

Hematites, silver.
Circa 1920.

4818 — 93ᵉ ANNÉE

6 JUILLET 1935

L'ILLUSTRATION

AUX GRANDES FÊTES DE PARIS : LA JOURNÉE DE LA VÉNERIE A BAGATELLE

Phot. J. Clair-Guyot. — Voir les pages 345 à 352 consacrées aux Fêtes de Paris.

Prix de ce numéro : **3 francs**

ÉTRANGER : Le prix de France majoré des frais de port.

13, RUE SAINT-GEORGES, PARIS (9ᵉ)

Voir au verso les tarifs d'abonnement.

Above: Enamel, silver. Circa 1910.
Opposite: *At the Paris Fairs: Hunt Day at Bagatelle.*
Cover of *L'Illustration,* 6 July 1935.

Above: Bakelite. Circa 1925.
Opposite: Eileen Gray, coromandel wood bench with amaranth
and lemonwood inlay (1920–1922). Valois Collection, Paris.

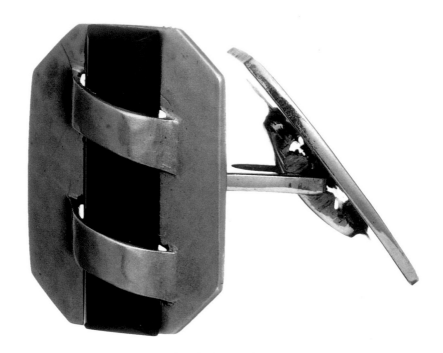

Onyx bar, beaten silver.
Jean Desprès, circa 1930.

Sapphires, white gold.
Circa 1925.

Opposite: Marlene Dietrich, 1934.

That scene, considered today as a classic of its kind, caused outrage at the time. Dietrich soon became an icon of lesbian chic, among women who drew inspiration from the audaciously original style that always remained uniquely hers. More than twenty years after *Morocco* was released, as she sang in London's *Café de Paris* in 1954, her admirers immediately recognized the cuff links she wore as a talisman. Her ambivalence was underlined by her voice, deeper and mistier than ever.

In England, Lady Una Trowbridge—in three-piece suit, tie, cuff links and aggressively flashing monocle—gave a different and still more radical interpretation of the androgynous woman. An intimate friend of Radclyffe Hall, the author of the sapphic novel *The Well of Loneliness*, she was also the inspiration for one of Romaine Brooks's best portraits—the force that emanates from the painting requires no comment.

And here is Churchill triumphantly gesturing his V for Victory, in the photograph that flashed around the world and has become a trophy for every cufflink collector. The pair chosen by Sir Winston forever links the headlong course of History to the far more frivolous history of masculine elegance.

Above: Lapis-lazuli, yellow gold.
Swiss craftsmanship, circa 1970.
Opposite: Sir Winston Churchill, 1945.

Enamel.
Lanvin, circa 1970.

Glass paste.
Maison Boyer, circa 1960.

Above: Silver. Cuff links worn by Air France
command pilots, circa 1960.
Opposite: Stewardess with a cosmonaut.

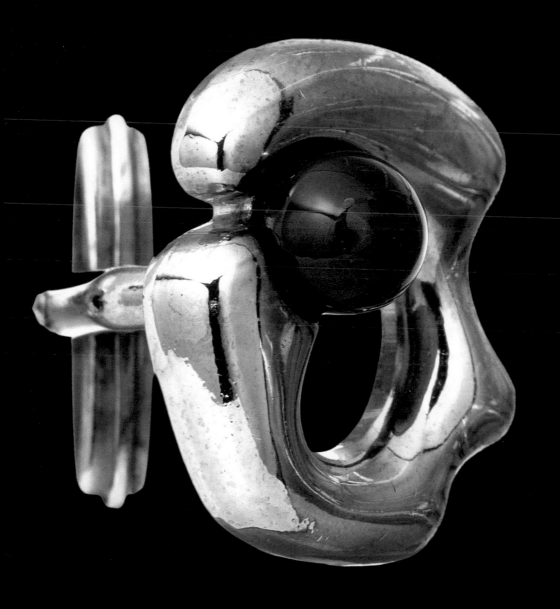

After the fashionably tasteful moderation of the postwar years, the second half of the 1960s saw inhibitions flying out of the window to open up the horizons of creativity—including among designers of cuff links. In tune with the swinging London scene, eccentricity became a must. The new Carnaby Street dandies—with Mick Jagger at the forefront—wore velvet and brocade, and the sassiest of them all used the men's makeup kit—kohl and lipstick—launched by Mary Quant.

Not since the 18th century had masculinity been more theatrical. Prince Raunitz, who, two hundred years earlier had been celebrated for his wasp-waisted satin corsets and would spend an hour every morning stepping through one salon after another, where footmen would throw clouds of powder of different colors into the air as he passed to create an exact nuance, would have been proud of such heirs. His modern descendants reveled in their outsized synthetic diamond cuff links in electric colors, with chain links extending right around their wrists like bracelets.

Above: Enamel, glass paste. Maison Boyer, circa 1960.
Opposite: Marianne Faithfull and Mick Jagger, 1969.
Preceding pages: Al Bartee at the Olympic Auditorium,
Los Angeles, 1951 (left). Garnets, yellow gold. Circa 1960 (right).

Amber, silver.
Russian craftsmanship, circa 1920.

Tiger's eye, silver.
Circa 1960.

Turquoise, yellow gold.
Circa 1930.

Wedgwood china.
England, circa 1950.

Glowing enamel, silver gilt.
Circa 1900.

Silver. Nefertiti,
circa 1950.

Agate, yellow gold,
silver. Spain.

Enamel. Cuff links worn by members
of the Bagatelle Polo Club, Paris.

Yellow gold, cabochon-cut
citrines. Circa 1950.

Opposite: Cameos in white and grey mother-of-pearl, silver. Circa 1920.

And so Cary Grant and his Saville Row flannels—the epitome of masculine elegance since the 1930s—gave way to new and more flamboyant idols, like Brett Sinclair in *The Persuaders,* the well-known TV series. Long hair artfully windblown, lace jabots, silk scarves in psychedelic prints, Op Art cuff links. Lord Sinclair, aka Roger Moore, was a worthy spiritual descendant of Prince Raunitz. Metamorphosing into James Bond and adopting a far more conventional style of dress, the actor was never without his cuff links, even in the most perilous situations. *Noblesse oblige.*

The 1970s saw cuff links gradually abandoned, as shirts increasingly came with ready-made buttons and buttonholes. Elegance was sacrificed to the functional, its sworn enemy. Yet some joined the resistance, refusing to capitulate. These aristocrats of the shirt-cuff—truly an international brotherhood of the cufflink—courageously asserted, echoing Baudelaire, "the need alas, all too rarely found today, to fight and destroy the trivial." Even the least wealthy among them would collect the round cuff links in plaited rayon invented by Charvet that were within reach of everyone's purse.

Tiger's eye, silver.
Lanvin, circa 1970.

Tiger's eye, silver.
Lanvin, circa 1970.

Opposite: Jack Nicholson at Mr Chow's. New York, 1980.

Synthetic stones, onyx.
Four pairs of American cuff links,
circa 1950.

Opposite: Nicolas Cage starring in *Face/Off*, 1997.
Preceding pages: A masked man at the Palace, Paris, 1978.
Elton John at a Cartier evening in Tunisia, 1983.

As sportswear and the slapdash became the rule in fashion, a new kind of imaginative, off-beat dandyism began to emerge, embodied to perfection by David Hockney and his London set. Immortalized by the cult film *A Bigger Splash*, which as we know caused one of the biggest splashes at the 1974 Cannes Film Festival, the English artist—complete with heavy glasses and tousled platinum blond hair—sported a combination of cuff links, spotted bow tie, chequered jacket and braces in primary colors, displaying them as often as he possibly could: at a preview at the Kasmin Gallery in New Bond Street, at a Quorum fashion parade, at Hollywood "arty-parties" or at a New York dinner party given by the curator Henry Geldzahler, who wore cuff links to sit for his portrait by Hockney. Likewise, his friend, the fashion designer Ossie Clark, creator of the hippie-glamour style with its weirdly whimsical prints designed by his wife Celia Birtwell wore cuff links from morning to night. With his "Jesus Christ Superstar" physique, Ossie Clark became an idol of the 1970s British youth scene.

Like Saint-Loup, who would never have dreamed of going out without his monocle, there are still some diehards today who simply would not survive without the creations of David Webb, Bulgari, Links—a London boutique that now attracts pilgrims from the world over—or David Brush who, turning to the ecological spirit of our times, has made a unique name for himself with his ingenuity in discovering alternatives to ivory. And there's Joël Rosenthal and his JAR label, now seen as one of the most inspired artists of his

The American writer Truman Capote. Italy, 1953.

generation. The sheer originality of form and combination displayed by JAR—in the designer's moonstone and gunmetal duo—could, single-handedly as it were, revitalize the art of the cufflink.

Lately, collectors seem to have acquired a fascination for vintage cuff links. Nothing is too rare or too original to adorn their shirt cuffs: shards of metal from a Viking axe, Toshikane masks or unique pieces designed forty or fifty years ago by Picasso, Dali or Calder. A lock of Marie-Antoinette's hair would of course be ideal, for exclusivity is more than ever de rigueur.

Above: Contemporary drawing by Lorenz Baümer.
Opposite: Rubies, grey gold. Mexico, circa 1950.

Calibrated sapphires, diamonds, white gold.
Van Cleef & Arpels, circa 1960.

Yellow gold, white gold,
rubies. Circa 1940.

Cabochon sapphires, yellow gold.
Schlumberger, 1960.

Cabochon sapphires,
white gold. Circa 1960.

Onyx, mother-of-pearl, yellow gold.
Swiss craftsmanship, circa 1970.

Above: Emeralds, yellow gold. Circa 1960.
Opposite: Nancy Cunard and Tristan Tzara, photographed
by Man Ray at a ball given by Count de Beaumont, 1924.

Citrines, yellow gold.
Bertrand Pizzin, 2000.

Chronology

17th century: The first cuff buttons appear, linked together with a chain. Most men were still content with ribbons or a simple piece of string to tie their shirts.

18th century: Still a rarity, cuff links were created as precious objects, in rose-cut diamonds or artificial gems known as *strass*.

19th century: Cuff links really came into their own from about 1850. The "swivel" system appeared, perfecting the classic chain and toggle devices.

1860: The advent of electroplating, combining gold or silver with other metals, contributes to the large-scale manufacture and distribution of gold or silver-plated cuff links.

1887: Creation of the Boyer establishment, which specialized in collar studs and removable shirtfronts (or "dickies") and broadened its range to include cuff links and tie pins. These were mainly in mother-of-pearl, pearls, enamel, miniature mosaic work, and precious or semiprecious stones, at a time when Tiffany, Wiese, Cartier and Fabergé reigned supreme over the world of masculine elegance. Today, the establishment works for designers such as Cardin, Dior, Lacroix and Saint-Laurent.

1900: Art Nouveau motifs are everywhere: profiles of women, garlands, irises and foliage. Lalique, Mucha and Guimard join the leading designers of the new century.

1920-1930: The Art Deco movement opens up the imagination of designers like Paul Brandt, Raymond Templier, Jean Desprès or René Boivin, to endless variations on abstract geometric motifs in enamel work. Famous fashion houses such as Cartier, Boucheron, Mellerio, Chaumet or Van Cleef & Arpels also turn to Art Deco for inspiration.

1924: Monsieur Boyer, of the Boyer establishment, creates the rod-type cufflink system, still the most widely used today, which is made up of a stud linked to a rod that swivels along its whole length between two stems.

1930: Press-stud cuff links come into fashion: these were two identical studs, often in enamel, mother-of-pearl or bakelite, closing tightly around the wrist.

1936: Van Cleef & Arpels invents the "channel setting" method whereby stones are set together with no visible metal support. The sapphires and rubies mounted in this way made perfect cuff links that are still manufactured today by the most renowned designers. Fulco di Verdura and Jean Schlumberger create their first designs for Haute Couture establishments like Chanel and Schiaparelli.

1940-1950: Cuff link designs become increasingly extravagant through the size and color of the gems used.

1940: Paul Flato creates a pair of platinum cuff links in the shape of the soles of four feet, for Adrian, the famous Hollywood fashion designer.

1950: Alexander Calder sculpts a pair of cuff links in the shape of two golden swirls, displayed today at the Calder Foundation.

1960-1970: Cuff links are increasingly adopted by fashion designers, often in voluminous shapes and featuring glass, gemstones and early designs in synthetic gems. Dior, Lanvin, Balmain and Cardin also draw inspiration from the age of rock & roll.

1975: Cartier designs heart-shaped cuff links in aquamarine with ruby pendants.

1976: Bulgari creates a design of diamond stars on a blue enamel background.

1975-1980: David Webb creates his fabulous bestiary: horses, frogs, unicorns and tigers with enamel faces and eyes in precious stones.

1980-1990: The classic look makes a comeback, as in these lapis-lazuli rods from Boucheron, previously created in the 1930s and worn by Marlene Dietrich. Studs with a "Zen" look from Dinh Van.

1990: A daring design from Jar: steel, diamonds and moonstones representing "night and day." Genuine mammoth-tusk ivory and lapis lazuli combine in a lavish jewel by David Brush.

2000: The younger generation rediscovers a taste for cuff links. Designs by Gucci. Paul Smith reinvents novelty cuff links to match his shirts. Cuff links become the latest craze from Colette, the new temple of trend-setting fashion.

Photo credits

Archives Valois, Paris: p. 46; Christie's: p. 12; Private collection/All rights reserved: p. 15, 16, 35; Culver Pictures, New York: p. 20; Galerie Sylvie Nissen, Paris: p. 63; Karl Lagerfeld: p. 5; Lorenz Baümer: p. 1, 72; Man Ray Trust/Adagp, Paris 2002: pp. 42, 77; Hermitage Museum, Saint Petersburg: p. 9; National Gallery, London: p. 10; Bob Willoughby: p. 56; Gnencioli/Cartier: p. 67; J. Clair-Guyot/L'Illustration: p. 44; Keiichi Tahara/Assouline: pp. 23, 27, 29, 33; Air France Museum/All rights reserved: p. 54; Philippe Sébirot/Assouline: pp. 11, 17, 19, 21, 22, 24, 25, 26, 28, 30, 31, 32, 34, 36, 37, 38, 39, 43, 45, 46, 48, 50, 52, 53, 55, 57, 58, 60, 61, 64, 69, 73, 74, 75, 76, 78; RMN/Hervé Lewandowski: pp. 14, 18; Robert Capa/Magnum Photo, Paris: p. 70; Roxanne Lowit/Assouline: pp. 65, 66; Rue des Archives/ AGIP: pp. 8, 51, 59, 62; Rue des Archives/BCA: p. 68; Rue des Archives/Everett: pp. 40, 41; Rue des Archives/TAL: p. 13; William Walling/Kobal Collection: p. 49.

Acknowledgements

Many thanks from Bertrand Pizzin to Karl Lagerfeld, for his beautifully written preface, which only a man of his talent, cultivation and elegance could have contributed to this book; to Lorenz Baümer, whose two creations designed for me are proof of his stature as the leading designer among the young generation of jewellers; to Jean-Michel Vincent, whose firm friendship persuaded me to write this book; to Pierre-Henri Vis-Derenne, a fellow antique-lover who never forgets his passion when out on treasure hunts.

Thanks from the publisher to Karl Lagerfeld, Lorenz Baümer, photographers Roxanne Lowit, Philippe Sébirot, Keiichi Tahara, Bob Willoughby, and the Air France Historic and Cultural Heritage Department, Cartier, Galerie Sylvie Nissen, RMN, Magnum Photo, Rue des Archives, Kobal Collection for their kind collaboration.